ਮੌਤਾਰ (ਉ) ਨੂੰ ਸ੍ਰੇਹ
ਸਾਹਿਤ ਦੇ ਸਹਾਇਕ,
June 1991

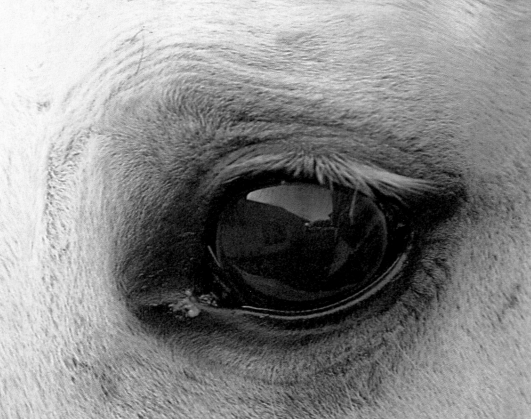

MAJESTY OF
THE HORSE

MAJESTY OF
THE HORSE

**MALLARD
PRESS**

An Imprint of BDD Promotional Book Company
666 Fifth Avenue
New York, N.Y. 10103

MALLARD PRESS
An imprint of
BDD Promotional Book Company, Inc.
666 Fifth Avenue
New York, N.Y. 10103

Mallard Press and its accompanying design and logo are
trademarks of BDD Promotional Book Company, Inc.

First published in the United States of America
in 1989 by Mallard Press

Printed and Bound in Spain

ISBN 0-792-45092-2

Text by Marietta Whittlesey
Captions by Rupert O. Matthews

Produced by and designed by Ted Smart
Photo Research: Edward Douglas, Natalie Goldstein and Annie Price
Editorial Assistance: Seni Glaister

It seems impossible to imagine a time when man and horse had not yet met. For the horse has been nearly as important as man himself in the civilization of the planet. It is difficult to imagine a world without the cooperation of the horse and his cousins the ass and mule, who were domesticated earlier but who never developed quite the following that *Equus caballus* did. Throughout history, the horse has been our companion, servant and partner. Those who had horses and could ride or drive them had the power to make his or her dreams come true. Small wonder that horses have always been prized.

Although horses were reintroduced into the New World by the Spanish conquistadors in the fifteenth and sixteenth centuries, it was in North America that one of the horse's primitive ancestors, eohippus, is believed to have originated. Some theories hold that the modern horse is not descended from one original ancestor but rather that four or five distinct types evolved separately in different parts of the world. The existence of the fossilized remains of early horses was instrumental in confirming Darwin's theory of evolution, which held that all horses were common descendants of eohippus. Fossils found in the United States date eohippus to about 55 million years ago. Also known as "dawn horse," this early progenitor of the magnificent hoofed creatures of today was a rather unprepossessing little creature, resembling a fox more than anything else. Standing between 10 and 20 inches (2.2 to 5 hands) high, eohippus had four toes in front and three behind, each with strong horny toenails, predecessors of hoofs, at the tip and, behind these, pads rather like those of a dog or cat. These tiny dawn horses became abundant in North America and eventually made their way to western Europe. When later the continents drifted farther apart, the descendants of these early horses in Europe and Asia diversified into a number of related animals, all of which became extinct about 40 million years ago. Back in North America, the more direct ancestors of the modern horse began to change to suit their environment. By 25 million years ago, their teeth had evolved to allow them to browse on soft plants. The forefeet lost their fourth toe, and the remaining side toes became more slender, so that more weight was borne on the middle toe of each foot, the horny central toe that we know as the hoof.

By seven million years ago, the last browsing horses became extinct and a totally new type of horse appeared. Although a time traveller might not recognize these animals as horses, they were beginning to develop attributes that we think of as typically equine. Teeth once suitable for browsing began to develop higher crowns with enameled ridges and a heavy coating of cement, making possible a diet of grasses that contained highly abrasive minerals. The feet lost their dog-like pads, and the weight of the little animal began to be carried almost entirely on the enlarged hoof of the central toe. When the horse ran, as he was increasingly forced to do to avoid predators, this central toe flexed and stretched a ligament that rebounded with each stride. Several types of these newly evolved three-toed horses came into existence on the grassy plains of North America. One of these groups, *hipparion*, is believed to have crossed into Asia and spread as far as Africa, where animals of this type had never before existed.

In North America, one final type of horse was beginning to develop: *Equus*, which is far more recognizable to us today than the earlier types. This is reflected in the scientific name for the modern horse, *Equus caballus*. The two side toes were now mere vestiges, and these horses moved on perfected versions of ligament-sprung hoofs. The various members of the *Equus* genus spread to South America and then to Asia, Europe and Africa as the last of the three-toed hipparion became extinct worldwide.

Domesticated horses are believed to have come from the wild horses of Eurasia. It is believed that most breeds of domesticated horses derived from *Equus caballus* while another closely related species, *Equus przewalskii*, native to Mongolia and the Gobi Desert, gave rise to the tarpan and other types of wild horse. One particularly compelling piece of modern evidence for several prehistoric horse ancestors rather than one is the fact that Przewalski horses have one chromosome more than all the other existing horse breeds. While examples of the Przewalski horse can still be found in some zoos, the last known tarpan became extinct at the end of the nineteenth century, the victim of rapacious hunting. The story goes that the last two remaining tarpans, a mare and her foal, were taken to the farm of a Russian count, Alexander Durilin, who hoped to use them in cross-breeding experiments. This wild mare, who had already lost one eye, managed to escape from her stall, fracturing a leg in the process. The leg was amputated, and the mare died two days later. The fate of her foal is not recorded. Although the true tarpan is extinct, similar-looking horses that were produced by selective breeding live in a preserve in Poland.

The modern horse is an intelligent creature whose extreme sensitivity and long memory enable him, in good hands, to be trained to extraordinary levels of accomplishment, ranging from high-level dressage to cutting. The same horse in bad hands can quickly be turned into an unmanageable renegade who ends badly.

Over the millennia of its long evolution in different environments, the horse has developed certain strong instincts. For instance, horses have an uncanny homing ability. Many a lost rider has been saved by dropping the reins and letting the horse make his own way back to the barn. Horses are said to have a stronger sense of smell than dogs. The horse's ability to detect water was of particular importance to horse-owning desert tribes, and this sense is most heavily developed in Arabian horses and their descendants.

The horse is able to sense the presence of hidden enemies, an instinct that persists somewhat out of proportion to the actual risks of modern-day life, as any rider who has spent a quarter of an hour trying to coax a nervous horse past a large rock can attest. Those who impugn the intelligence of the horse because he is easily "spooked" don't know the origins of this behavior. Primitive horses were prey to larger animals on the open plains and so learned to react quickly and run the moment they sensed danger. American Indians knew of this ability and relied upon their horses to alert them to trouble rather than post guards at night.

There are those who believe that many pack and herd animals, such as wolves and horses, have developed a high degree of telepathic ability, enabling them to communicate with members of the herd over a wide area. Many accomplished riders also seem to have this ability to communicate with their mounts on some silent level well beyond the usual leg, weight and hand aids, so that horse and rider truly appear to act and move as one being.

Unlike the young of other domesticated animals, which are born nearly blind and relatively helpless, the newborn horse, called a foal, just about hits the ground running. Again, this innate ability harkens back to his evolution on the open plains. The spindly foal usually lurches to its feet, eyes wide open, and begins to nurse within an hour of birth. Within several hours the new foal has figured out how to keep his long legs underneath him well enough to stay by his dam. Like the young of many other large mammals, the foal is born with an instinct to stay by the legs he sees first—usually those of his mother. This also was an important instinct for herd animals to develop to keep their young from straying and becoming adopted by other mothers who might not have milk to feed them.

The foal is weaned at anywhere from six months to a year, depending upon his development. His first year is relatively uneventful—learning to be handled, haltered and led, and having his hoofs trimmed by a farrier. For the well-bred foal there may be breeders' shows where he will be shown in halter at his mother's side.

If he is a Thoroughbred, he is officially a yearling on January 1 following his birth—even if he is really only seven or eight months old. For the Quarter Horse and some other breeds, the official birthday is April 1. The young horse is now called a filly if a female and a colt if a male. By this time, the horse's body has caught up with his legs and he looks quite a bit more like a mature horse. Life is still fairly uncomplicated for a yearling if he's lucky. If he is not, his owner may already be using him for work or riding. Even though a big yearling may stand nearly as high as an adult horse, he is still a baby whose bones are forming. To put a horse to work too early is begging for later unsoundness and a shortened working life. At the other end of the scale, the Lipizzaners of the Spanish Rid-

ing School of Vienna are not even started until about age four and don't usually begin to perform for audiences until they have had many more years of schooling. This long maturation period seems to pay off since these horses are routinely able to keep performing well into their twenties movements that require strength and agility beyond the capacity of many of the fittest of younger horses.

By his second year the young horse will probably begin his education. While schooling methods and timetables vary according to what the horse is to be used for and the trainer's personal philosophy, most riding horses are started off either by being lunged (worked in a circle on a long line) or driven in long reins with the rider walking behind. Lungeing helps to develop balance and agility and obedience. At this stage the horse will also be taught voice commands. Part of this year's program will also be to familiarize him with the feel of the bit in his mouth. A very gentle bit, often with moving parts to encourage him to mouth the bit and play with it, is introduced. If he is to be a riding horse, he is familiarized with the saddle. He is first introduced to the idea of being mounted by having the rider lie quietly across the saddle while being led by an assistant. After this no longer worries him, the rider climbs gently into the saddle. This is usually done toward the end of the second year in order to lay the groundwork for the next year when mounted work will begin in earnest.

By the time he is three the young horse is beginning to be taught the basics, such as balancing himself with a rider aboard and understanding the leg, weight and hand aids. Once these fundamentals are understood, the young horse is ready to make a pleasant riding animal or to go on to more specialized training for a particular sport.

It was sometime between 30,000 B.C. and 10,000 B.C. that man first became attracted to the wild horses around him. In those millennia, human beings were hunter-gatherers, and horses were an important source of food. The ancient wall paintings found in the limestone caves of the Pyrenees, of horses being killed by arrows and of pregnant mares, were probably created to ensure success in hunting, since primitive humans tended to worship as the life-giving source of nourishment the animals they killed and ate. It wasn't until the Neolithic period that humans devised the mechanical means, such as leather thongs and knots, to capture and subjugate animals as large as the horse. The vines available to Paleolithic man were sufficient to master dogs but nothing larger.

There is no agreement about who first domesticated the horse, and where. Some authorities feel that horses were first used in Mongolia as early as 5000 B.C. because people in this area of Asia had first domesticated the reindeer, which they used to pull sledges, to drive and ride, and for food and leather. Perhaps it was they who first tamed the wild horses around them as a substitute for reindeer. It has even been suggested that the first horses to be tamed were easy-to-catch orphaned foals who were raised by reindeer mothers whose milk is digestible by foals. Chinese ceramics that date to 3500 B.C. clearly depict ridden and driven horses.

Recent thinking on the domestication of animals holds that horses and other animals that man domesticated were not unwilling captives so much as co-beneficiaries. In return for servitude to man, horses were spared the difficulties of survival in the wild. An expert on animal domestication at the British Museum, Juliet Clutton-Brock, points out that as the climate warmed after the Ice Age, what once had been vast open plains became dense forests, unsuitable for horses. The large packs of wild horses declined to near-extinction and would have vanished if they had not been domesticated and put under the protection of humans.

Some authorities claim that the early domesticators of the horse used it for both riding and driving, but that in many cases horses were predominantly driven animals because of their small stature. Certainly the invention of the wheel during the Bronze Age made travel or hauling goods by wagon practical. The first saddles, at least in the Near East, were probably invented by the Assyrian cavalry, since bas reliefs of Assyrian archers show them riding with padded saddle cloths, bridles with bits and even something that looks like a martingale and breastplate, used to hold the saddle in place. (There is also controversy as to whether the Huns of Mongolia or the Hindus should be credited with the invention of stirrups.)

The Hittites saw the merits of having horses pull their war chariots and it is from their culture that we have the earliest known manual of horse training: clay tablets written in the second century B.C. for the instruction of charioteers. Despite its archaic packaging, the information it presents is surprisingly modern, detailing the progressive training of a horse over a six-month period as well as matters of stable management and horse care.

THE WORKING HORSE

IN WAR AND CONQUEST

Horses have had a long and, as more sophisticated weaponry was invented, increasingly tragic history in mankind's wars. The horse was first used in warfare about 5000 B.C. by the Mongolian cavalry. Riding small, sturdy descendants of local wild horses, the Mongolian archers could shoot with deadly accuracy at a full gallop. These early cavalrymen lived in close contact with their horses, drinking mare's milk and making from it a liquor known as kummis, which is still drunk in parts of eastern Eurasia. It was during the repeated Mongolian invasions that the horse was introduced into China and with it the Mongols'

knowledge of horse management and the use of equipment such as saddles and horse collars. By 1200 B.C. chariot warfare had spread to Egypt and Persia, where archers in horse-drawn, light weight chariots could easily decimate armies on foot.

The idea of a mounted cavalry soon spread. Persia under Xerxes had 80,000 chariots and ridden horses. Horses were being specially bred for war. No longer were the shaggy little 13-hand-high Mongolian ponies adequate. The Nicaeans were breeding faster horses that stood 14 to 15 hands, and their breeding stock was in great demand. The early cavalry charges must have been utterly terrifying for the unmounted infantry, since the horse soldiers were usually mounted on stallions specially schooled to encourage all their natural aggression. History has not recorded how much fighting went on among horses whose riders were allies but whose own aggressions knew no such allegiance.

One of the most famous early horsemen was the Spartan officer Xenophon, who wrote extensively on the selection, breeding and schooling of horses for the cavalry. It is no exaggeration to say that his principles of equine body dynamics, equitation and horse psychology still influence us today. He taught patience and kindness rather than pain and fear in the handling and training of horses. "The one best precept," he said, "the Golden Rule in dealing with a horse, is never to approach him angrily." Xenophon understood very well the importance of balancing and suppling work, of teaching horses to move off their hocks and to carry themselves with lightness. Although he did not have the benefit of a saddle, Xenophon can be credited with developing the basic stock seat used today. "I do not approve of the seat as in a chair," he wrote, "but that which is like a man standing upright with his legs apart." Such a position, he felt, gave a better grip of the horse and hence a better foundation from which to hurl a javelin.

By the eleventh century, as civilization moved westward, the type of horse favored for war had changed again. Horses were slowly becoming larger and heavier, probably due to the influence of northern and alpine types that were descendants of the Roman pack horses (themselves descendants of the Stone Age horses of western Europe), with some Andalusian blood mixed in. Ancestors of most of today's draft breeds, these horses were hefty cob types still about 14 hands, but extremely strong and rugged, with feet as hard as diamonds. When William the Conqueror invaded England in A.D. 1066, his army was mounted on these heavy horses.

In some parts of the world, however, the shaggy Mongolian ponies reigned supreme. As recently as the thirteenth century A.D., Sabutai led a cavalry about 150,000 strong that had been assembled by Genghis Khan and laid siege to Asia and eastern Europe until they were stopped at what is modern-day Poland.

The knights in armor that we associate with medieval Europe actually had their origin among the Byzantines, superb horsemen who fought on horses sheathed in armor. With the introduction of stirrups, a different type of warfare became possible. Now a soldier had the option of throwing or thrusting a spear, or of standing braced in his stirrups and charging at an opponent with his spear or lance held under his arm. Because such lancers could pierce an oak door several inches thick, chain mail gave way to heavy plate armor to protect the body. The horses used by the medieval knights had to be bred heavier not only to carry the 600-pound load of a knight in his unyielding armor, but also to pack more power behind the lance. Hence the name "charger." These horses didn't really charge in the same way that later cavalry horses charged. In fact, the fast gait for these war horses was the amble, occasionally a trot, which was probably all the poor overladen creatures could manage. Nonetheless, they were expected to prance and pirouette in tournaments and exhibitions, their obedience commanded by means of rather brutal bits and spurs. Probably the riders had no real idea of the cruelty of some of their methods or of the sensitivity of the horse, for these chargers were a knight's proudest possession and, as today, a symbol of nobility and riches.

By the seventeenth century other changes had taken place in warfare and, accordingly, in war horses. With the invention of firearms and artillery, the cavalry became a more elite (and usually aristocratic) corps that used fast horses for making swift, surprise attacks, although armies still used large numbers of pack and draft animals. The English Thoroughbred, a product of the native English mares and one of the three Arab foundation sires, or one of their descendants, was larger and faster still. The introduction of this breed made possible a different type of cavalry capable of sudden blitzkriegs. There were essentially three types of cavalry. The dragoon rode horses from position to position, but generally fired from the ground or from the halt. Lancers rode faster horses and attacked from horseback. The fastest and most dramatic were hussars, who formed their line out of sight and range of the enemy and suddenly attacked, wielding pistols, swords or lances. Napoleon was finally routed at Waterloo largely as a result of the attack by Blücher's Prussian hussars.

It was Cortes, De Soto and the other Spanish conquistadors who reintroduced horses to the New World in the late fifteenth century. The horses, of Arab and Andalusian stock, were shipped over in slings in the holds of ships, surely a nightmare trip for man and beast alike! Prior to their arrival, there had been no native horses in the Americas for millions of years. Certainly the Aztecs had never seen horses, and when they first saw the Spanish gentlemen astride the creatures, they thought the two were one omnipotent beast.

Some of the most celebrated horse-and-rider partnerships in history began in wartime. One of the most famous of these was that between General Robert E. Lee and his grey gelding, Traveller. Many accounts tell of the mystical bond between Lee and this Tennessee Walking Horse. Lee himself wrote, "A poet . . . could . . . depict his worth and describe his endurance of toil, hunger, thirst, heat and cold and the dangers and sufferings through which he passed. He could dilate upon his sagacity and affection and his invariable response to every wish of his rider." Other such great partnerships have included those between Alexander the Great and Bucephalus and Stonewall Jackson and Little Sorrel.

By the early eighteenth century, the various tribes of Plains Indians had their own extremely effective version of a cavalry, mounted mostly on wild mustangs descended from Spanish stock. The Indians tended to be neglectful horsemasters, with the exception of Nez Percé Indians, however, who helped develop the Appaloosa breed. It is said that the Comanches, who lived close to their horses and were superb riders, were possessed of a light cavalry the equal of any in the world. They rode on imitations of Spanish saddles complete with stirrups, or else they rode bareback. A thong hitched around the horse's lower jaw served as bit and bridle. One of the Indians' most impressive feats was to drop down by their galloping horse's shoulder—one leg across his back, one hand holding on to a thong braided into his mane—and shoot arrows under the horse's neck or over his back, protected from the enemy.

Although several modern countries such as China, India and the Soviet Union still maintain cavalry divisions, World War II saw the last major cavalry charges. These occurred mostly on the eastern front where the Germans were repeatedly attacked by Russian cavalry which, like their Mongol forebears of seven thousand years earlier, were mounted on hardy Steppes ponies. They were able to stage sudden attacks and then gallop off while German tanks stood frozen and buried in snow.

Yet one of the most tragic charges of the war was that made near Moscow by the 44th Mongolian cavalry division. Two thousand horsemen, sabers drawn, charged the German 106th Infantry division with its modern artillery and small arms. Line after line of brave horses and riders were gunned down in the snow before they even reached enemy lines.

Thankfully, such tragic slaughters convinced military strategists that horses had no place in modern warfare and the noble horse is no longer forced to suffer the terror of the battlefield to aid humans in solving their differences.

IN THE CITY AND COUNTRY

The work done by horses throughout the ages includes pulling farm equipment, drawing a variety of private and commercial wagons and carriages, pulling barges, working in coal mines, performing numerous functions on ranches and carrying mounted policemen.

Although horses were used as draft and pack animals, oxen were actually the preferred work animals for a long time. Bronze Age cave paintings that show horses pulling plows are said actually to depict just the first day of the growing season when horses drew the first furrow. Man hoped that horses, who were believed to embody the spirit of the seed, would ensure good crops. The day-to-day farm chores were performed by steadier, stronger oxen, who were cheaper to keep and made excellent meat. This was true until the Middle Ages when horses large enough to replace oxen at certain chores were beginning to be decommissioned as war horses. Prior to this, medieval Great Horses were prized as war animals and the thought of harnessing them to do an ox's work would have seemed absurd. Their numbers were also limited by the amount of grazing available, for it takes plenty of good-quality acreage to support these big horses. It wasn't until the invention of firearms, which could pierce armor, that these knights' horses were replaced by faster, handier horses who could participate in hit-and-run attacks.

The peacetime use of heavy horses was also facilitated by the invention of the horse collar, which permitted the animal to put his full weight into the work without having his breathing restricted by the older breastplate type of harness.

Although some horses were used in agriculture prior to the harnessing of the large draft horses, they were used mostly for such purposes as grinding grain or operating wine or olive presses. It wasn't until the eighteenth century that heavy draft horses were used as farm horses. Various draft horse breeds had been developed in different countries, but all had as a common ancestor the heavy Norman horses mixed later with Arab blood. These, interbred with local types, gave rise to the characteristic breeds of each country: the Shires and Clydesdales of Britain, the Percherons and Ardennais of France, the Brabants of Belgium. Selective breeding and improved nutrition made these horses stronger and more plentiful.

The late eighteenth century saw the beginning of mechanization in farming. Enormous teams of twenty-five or thirty mules or horses were needed to pull these new mowing and reaping machines. Horses were also used extensively in logging operations to pull felled trees out of the woods. Draft horses and mules flourished in agriculture until this century, particularly in places such as the Great Plains of the United States, western Canada and Australia with their vast expanses of grainfields and grasslands.

More recently still, there has been a renewed interest in the use of draft horses in farming and logging. This can be seen at any country fair where the horse pulls are usually one of the main attractions. The rise in prices for oil and farm machinery has made some smaller scale farmers return to draft horses to work the land. Although its costs quite a lot to feed and maintain one of these big horses, they are a good deal more pleasant to work around than modern farm machinery and, in some cases, they do their job far better than machines. Horse-drawn harrows are still superior to those drawn by machine, because the horses don't compact the soil as they tread upon it. Horses are superior to trucks for getting around in the woods, particularly in the snow, and hauling out logs or buckets of maple sap. Horses are also a valuable source of fertilizer that is much prized by organic farmers and gardners.

Another early job for the working horse was pulling a variety of passenger coaches. Queen Elizabeth I may have originated the idea about 400 years ago when she began to travel about her domain in a wagon pulled by a team of six or eight horses. Again, these were the massive descendants of the medieval knights' war horses, since only horses of exceptional size and strength could have managed to pull such heavy loads through the rutted, muddy tracks that constituted the roads of the time.

The idea caught on, and by the beginning of the seventeenth century, passenger and freight coaches drawn by horses became commonplace. Because of the bad roads, however, this method of transport was slower than the ridden horse. By the beginning of the last century, the roads of Europe and North America had greatly improved and also increased in number. Phaetons, broughams, gigs, victorias, surreys, buckboards, and governess carts jammed the streets and roadways, providing at least as much pleasure to their owners as automobiles do today.

Before the advent of roads and railways, mail and messages were delivered by horseback messenger services. One of the earliest was that of the Praetorian Guard, which was established by the Romans. Its messengers made the trip from Rome to London over rough country in five days—a feat even when accomplished by modern automobile! The first horse-drawn mail coach was established in 1784 and ran between London and Bath, England. By the close of the century, there were forty-two mail coach routes in Great Britain, creating a network of staging posts and coaching inns where tired horses could be exchanged at regular intervals.

In the United States, the mail was delivered first by horseback riders and later by stagecoach. The Pony Express was a private company which in 1860 inaugurated service between St. Joseph, Missouri, and Sacramento, California, to accommodate the westward movement brought about by the Gold Rush. Not unlike the system set up in England, the Pony Express had relay stations along the route where tired horses were exchanged for fresh horses. The fastest time the express ever made was in 1861. It took seven days, seventeen hours to transport President Lincoln's Inaugural Address. For less urgent dispatches, the company guaranteed to cover the

1,966 miles of the full route in ten days.

In the United States, the horse was instrumental in opening the West and in helping to make large fortunes for some of the cattle ranchers who had settled there. Although we tend to think of the era of longhorn cattle and cowboys as a peculiarly American phenomenon, almost everything that we think of as "Western" (from the style of farming to the saddles and, in some cases, the vocabulary) was actually introduced by Cortes and his followers, who were familiar with the large cattle ranches of Spain and Portugal.

The horses used in the West were of two types—the mustang, descendants of Cortes's horses and their relatives, and the Quarter Horse, brought from Virginia and the Carolinas where the breed was developed in Colonial times to work and to run a phenomenally fast quarter-mile (or less) on the short, straight tracks that the settlers had cleared from the woods. As more and more Thoroughbreds were imported from England, Quarter Horse racing began to die out in the East, but by then Quarter Horses were moving westward. They were most happily received, for they were perfect for the jobs required of them. These original Quarter Horses were stocky and muscular with short necks and short legs. Their immense speed over a short distance enabled them to chase runaway steers. Their short, strong backs and powerful hindquarters gave them the maneuverability that they needed to help cowboys cut and rope calves or to brace themselves against roped steers who were nearly their equal in size and weight. Their strong legs and tough feet carried them over uneven, rocky terrain that would have been torturous for finer, frailer horses.

Today, ranching still goes on in much the same way on the enormous cattle and sheep stations of Australia where stockmen riding sturdy Walers, which were first developed for the British cavalry in India, carry on the age-old jobs of checking fences, carrying food to livestock and herding and driving animals. The working saddle horse is still employed in numbers in the Rhône delta in southwestern France. There cowboys, known as *guardiens,* capture the wild black bulls that are exported to countries where bullfighting is still popular. The preferred mount of the *guardien* is the Camargue, a type of indigenous wild horse.

In England during the Industrial Revolution, before the advent of the railroads, a system of canals provided the fastest way to transport raw materials and finished products throughout the country. Draft horses on towpaths alongside the canals pulled the barges laden with goods. Similar systems operated in other countries as well. Even after the railroads came, horses were still needed to pull fire engines and a variety of passenger and freight coaches. The occasional draft horse lingered on in most cities of Europe and North America until quite recently. As late as the mid-1960's several privately owned draft horses could be seen on the streets of New York City. One was an old sorrel whose owner sold plants and small potted trees door to door. Another, a smart hackney, used to be driven through the streets by the owner of a successful East Side bar. Nowadays, New York, like many cities, still has horse-drawn carriages as a tourist attraction. Efforts are being made, however, to restrict the use of these horses, as it is clear that modern-day city streets are not a safe or pleasant environment for horses.

IN CEREMONY

When properly trained and cared for, the horse has about him an aristocratic air that is unmatched by any other animal, domesticated or wild. The arched neck, the intelligent eyes, the carefully placed hooves all bespeak an innate proudness that makes the horse an important part of ceremonial occasions. Naturally, this was true in the days when horses were the only means of transportation and conveyance, but even in modern times, there are ceremonies which would be lackluster indeed without the presence of horses.

An example of twentieth-century ceremonial horses familiar to most Americans are the horses of the Old Guard stationed at Fort Meyer, Virginia, adjacent to Arlington National Cemetery. These horses participate in the funerals of American Presidents and high-ranking government officials and military officers. Horses of this unit also have the happier duty of entertaining crowds in various military shows, such as the Twilight Tatoo, performed weekly during the summer at the Jefferson Memorial.

Those of us old enough to recall the funeral of President Kennedy will never forget the sight of the riderless black horse with the boots fixed backwards in the stirrups, symbolic of a slain leader, as part of the solemn procession that made its way through the streets of Washington to Arlington. This horse was named Black Jack after General John J. "Black Jack" Pershing, the World War I hero. In his twenty-four-year career with the Old Guard, Black Jack participated in the funerals of three other Presidents and many notable personages. Black Jack was retired to pasture at Fort Meade, Maryland, where he was feted annually on his birthday with his favorite, a 25-pound butter pecan cake, and presents from admirers countrywide.

Horses figure prominently in many state occasions in Great Britain, a nation of horse lovers. The annual Trooping the Colours, performed on the Queen's official birthday in June, is a glorious military pageant in which the Queen takes the salute, attended by members of her family and by the Horse Guards.

The wedding day of Princess Diana and Prince Charles called forth the British ceremonial horse in great numbers. Members of the Household Cavalry escorted the various carriages in the wedding procession through the streets of London. Lady Diana Spencer rode to St. Paul's in the

Glass Coach, used for nearly all royal weddings since 1910, so that well-wishers could easily glimpse the bride. The carriage was drawn by two bays and was escorted by members of the Mounted Branch of the Metropolitan Police. The bridegroom in his landau was drawn by four matched grey Oldenburgs, resplendent in silver mane dressings and caparison, while the Queen rode in an open, semi-state landau drawn by four greys and escorted by Life Guard outriders.

The Royal Canadian Mounted Police, founded in 1873, no longer has horses on active duty. What remains, however, is the famous musical ride, performed for the pleasure of audiences the world over by the red-coated Mounties on matched black horses.

THE HORSE IN SPORT

EQUITATION

After Xenophon's treatise on horsemanship and the art of riding, there was a sort of dark age during which riders (at least in Britain and on the Continent) made no particular effort to accommodate themselves to their horses. The chargers of the Middle Ages performed rather advanced movements by any standard but these were obtained by the use of vicious curb bits and sharp spurs rather than by the natural methods favored by Xenophon.

It wasn't until the Renaissance in Italy in the sixteenth century that riding came to be regarded as an art comparable to painting or music and an essential part of every noble's education. Members of the aristocracy revived the movements that they believed the knights in armor would have used in battle—movements such as the piaffe and the croupade and the airs above ground that are familiar to us from the exhibitions given by the Spanish Riding School of Vienna and the Cadre Noir of the French Cavalry School at Saumur in France.

There were many masters of equitation during this period—Grisone and Pignatelli in Italy, Pluvinel in France—and it would be impossible to do justice to their individual contributions to the art of classical equitation in so short a space. In general, it can be said that each of these masters was influential and transformed riding from the unstudied utilitarian approach of the Middle Ages into the amalgam of physiology, psychology and physics that it still is today for serious riders.

In 1559 Fiaschi, while recommending that animals be treated patiently, still advised that recalcitrant animals could be made to go forward by tying cats to their tails or by digging sharp hooks into their hindquarters. It should be mentioned that the horses he was working with were the heavy, coldblooded descendants of the medieval war horses and not the Arabs and Andalusians that were just beginning to come into vogue for classical riding and who could hardly have pros-

pered under such fierce practices.

By 1623, when Pluvinel was teaching King Louis XIII of France to ride, he was advocating suppling exercises before asking the horse to perform difficult movements—something that no modern dressage rider would ever neglect but a real innovation three and a half centuries ago! Likewise, Pluvinel understood the importance of the hindquarters in correct movement at a time when most attention was directed toward cranking the head and neck into a fixed position by means of artificial aids zealously applied. Pluvinel is believed to be the first trainer to have used stationary pillars for training horse and rider to perform airs above the ground. Work between pillars is still on the program of the Spanish Riding School's performances.

The modern era of horsemanship can probably be said to have begun with François Robichon de la Guérinière, often called the father of classical equitation. His book, *Ecole de Cavalerie* (Cavalry School), is still revered at the Spanish Riding School. Many of de la Guérinière's innovations form the basis of schooling today. He invented the shoulder-in and other lateral movements still used for suppling a horse and teaching him to use his body correctly. He taught his students to sit in a relaxed, balanced seat and to use the legs, seat and hand aids in concert, but subtly so that they were not apparent to the observer. De la Guérinière was humane in his approach to horses. He understood that not all horses have the same physical ability to do everything that is asked of them and that training methods must be individualized. He condemned the use of force and cruelty in training, emphasizing that the well-schooled horse must perform willingly. De la Guérinière was also the first to use advanced dressage movements in the schooling of war horses.

Another major change that de la Guérinière brought about was in the saddles used for school riding. The high pommel and cantle necessary to keep the rigid, armored knights in place were lowered, and knee and thigh rolls were added to stabilize the leg. The saddles used in performances by the Spanish Riding School today are quite similar to those introduced by de la Guérinière.

Anywhere there are jumping competitions in the world today, you will see the influence of a turn-of-the-century Italian cavalry officer named Federico Caprilli. Caprilli revolutionized equitation, particularly over fences. Before Caprilli's system was adopted, the predominant teaching held that it was extremely difficult for the horse to raise his forehand in the air and to get it over a jump. The response to this perceived problem was actually a total hindrance to the horse's natural way of going. In order to make it easier for the horse, riders leaned as far back as they could, to unweight the horse's forehand, and pulled upwards with their hands to help further pick the forehand up over the fence. Photographs of pre-Caprilli riders going over jumps show a horrible picture of distressed horses, gripped firmly between their rider's legs, their backs hollowed, their heads yanked back so far that they are virtually unable to see the fences, while the riders are leaning their full weight back on the horse's hindquarters. Caprilli, who had carefully observed the horse's movement at each gait and over fences, set about improving the seat and analyzing how the horse could be supported and encouraged to work obediently without suffering and without needless expenditure of effort. Although he met with much opposition, one of his superiors at the Tor di Quinto cavalry school in Pinerole finally agreed to let Caprilli work with thirty students. After only a few months, a review board noted a difference between Caprilli's pupils and those taught according to traditional methods, but it still took some time to convince the old guard at the school of the superiority of Caprilli's system.

Caprilli taught that the rider's weight should be carried in the heels and the stirrups shortened to permit better balance. Instead of throwing themselves backwards and pulling the horse's head up in the air while going over fences, he taught his riders to follow the movement of the horse's head and neck with their hands while staying forward off the back. This permitted the horse to use the strength of his hindquarters to push himself up and over the fence without the encumbrance of the rider's weight. The use of a snaffle bit rather than the previously used double bridle more appropriate to advanced dressage encouraged the horse to stretch his neck and back. Once allowed this freedom, the horse had no need of the rider's help in raising his forehand, for that work could be carried out naturally by the hindquarters. The enormous difference between the old system and Caprilli's can be seen in the photographs of Caprilli and his followers clearing very large fences with ease, looking very much like riders of today.

SHOW JUMPING

Show jumping is a test of the horse's ability to jump large fences. Except for the cross-country phase of the combined training event, show jumping is probably the most exciting for the spectator and also the easiest to understand: the horse who knocks down the least number of fences within the shortest time, if the competition is timed, and with the fewest disobediences, is the winner.

Jumping wasn't commonplace until the Enclosure Acts of the mid-eighteenth century in England permitted the building of fences around agricultural lands, which then forced fox hunters to jump from field to field. Naturally, soon enough, there began to be jumping competitions to see whose horse could jump best, a welcome accompaniment to the long-established competitions to see whose horse was fastest.

In the 1860's, in Dublin, for example, competitions were held over a single vertical with rails and hedges or a wide jump over an expanse of water with a hedge at the take-off point. One competition held in Paris at that time was more like a modern horse trial than show jumping since the horses were paraded in the ring and then ridden out to jump a course of natural fences in the countryside. At the horse show at the Agricultural Hall in Islington, London, in 1876, horses who were already showing in in-hand classes were eligible to enter "leaping classes"—as they were called then—which were much more like modern-day hunter classes. The horses were judged by a Master of Foxhounds on the basis of their form over fences rather than on their jumping ability only. By 1883, the National Horse Show was established at Madison Square Garden in New York. Despite the prevalence of the pre-Caprilli seat, these horses and riders jumped some big fences by any standards. An unofficial record of 8 feet 2 inches set in 1902 by the Thoroughbred Heatherbloom, ridden by Dick Donnelly, still stands today.

By the 1950's the military influence was much less evident, and women began to appear in the Olympics and in other top international competitions. Pat Smythe of Great Britain, aboard Flanagan, was the first woman rider to compete in the Olympics. Her team brought home the bronze. Nowadays, women are a common sight in all levels of show jumping. Today's stars include Melanie Smith, winner of a team gold in the 1984 Olympics riding the Dutch warmblood Calypso, and Katie Monahan Prudent and Leslie Burr Lenehan, two top child riders who never stopped riding. Gail Greenough of Canada beat out all the competition in the finals of the 1986 World Championships. This competition is particularly difficult, as each of the four finalists must ride not only his or her own horse but also those of the other three top finalists over a short but difficult course. Greenough, then only twenty-six years old and riding in her first World Championship, amazed spectators and fellow riders alike with her four perfect rounds, beating out Conrad Holmfeld and Abdullah, winners of the silver at the 1984 Olympics, as well as Nick Skelton, England's leading professional, and Pierre Durand of France, who later won the individual gold at Seoul in 1988.

While local show jumping competitions at horse shows are open to both amateur and professional riders, for a long time the International Olympic Committee barred professional horsemen from competing in international events. Beginning in the 1960's, it became possible to regain amateur status and so international competitions— excluding the Olympics—were opened to professionals. As of 1986, professionals may even ride in the Olympics, but they may only claim amateur status for a competition once. Since many open jumper riders in the United States and Great Britain are professionals, this relaxation of the rules has made it possible for professionals like Rodney Jenkins of the United

States, Nelson Pessoa of Brazil, David Broome of Great Britain, and Eddie Macken of Ireland to represent their countries.

Unlike dressage, where the horse's physique can't help but be significant, the open jumper need not be a perfect physical specimen. It is thus a sport with its share of Cinderella stories. One of the most heartwarming is that of the wonderful grey, Snow Man, who was saved from slaughter by Harry de Leyer. De Leyer was at the time the head riding instructor at a private girls' school on Long Island, New York. After restoring the horse to health, de Leyer put Snow Man to work as a school horse for the girls to ride and as a pleasure horse for his family. Soon, however, Snow Man began to amuse himself by jumping out of the paddock and de Leyer realized that Snow Man had real jumping talent. Snow Man, who was bought for eighty dollars, won countless competitions and was named Horse of the Year. At the opposite end of the spectrum are some of today's big stars like Calypso, who are so expensive that they are owned by syndicates.

Jumpers can be of any breeding. Thoroughbreds are natural athletes and have long dominated the field. However, various types of warmbloods are very much in vogue right now as sport horses, and Quarter Horses and crossbreds of various kinds are also seen.

DRESSAGE

The word *dressage* derives from the French *dresser,* "to train." Originally it just meant "training," but nowadays it is a very popular sport in itself. Like other equestrian sports, dressage competitions have many levels, so that horses and riders compete against others at their level who are performing the same test. The lowest-level competitions, training, first level and second through fourth levels, are closer to the original meaning of *dressage,* since the required movements, at least through second level, do not surpass anything that the very well-schooled riding horse should be able to execute. (As an aside it should be mentioned that the movements of dressage were developed from the horse's natural movements while at play.)

The next levels, Prix St. Georges, Intermediare and Grand Prix, are international levels where dressage becomes much more specialized. Although these competitions do not call for the airs above the ground, they are much closer to the classical school riding of the seventeenth century. Dressage horses at the higher levels are specialists whose muscle development and carriage are quite different from those of comparably advanced jumpers or eventers, and most would no longer be suitable for these sports.

Dressage competitions consist of programed rides called tests, which the competitors must memorize. The tests, which are designed and published by the American Horse Shows Associ-

ation, stay in effect for a couple of years at a time so that horses and riders have ample time to perfect their rides.

Competitions take place in an arena 20 meters wide and 60 meters long surfaced with sand, grass or an artificial footing such as Fibar. Around the arena are markers with letters which the rider must memorize since they are not in alphabetical sequence. There are also a series of unmarked points within the arena demarcating the center of the ring, the center line and other internal points.

At the beginning of the test, the rider has a couple of minutes to ride around the outside of the ring. When the bell rings, the competitor enters the ring, halts at a given point and salutes. Then the test proceeds. The test is scored by one or more judges at different positions around the ring, assisted by a scribe to whom the judge dictates his impressions and scores so that he needn't take his eyes off the horse.

At the most basic level, the test asks for simple figures such as large circles, diagonal lines and changes of direction performed at all three gaits (walk, trot and canter). At the higher levels, more advanced work such as flying changes of lead, lateral movements (in which the horse goes both sideways and ahead) at all three gaits, counter-canter, and collections and extensions at different gaits are asked and more accuracy is required. At all levels, several different aspects of the test are judged. First of all, each movement is judged and scored from 1 to 10 on quality and accuracy.

Dressage done correctly looks so elegant and effortless that it belies the enormous strength and concentration required of both horse and rider, not to mention the long years of schooling. Dressage requires constant communication between horse and rider that takes years to master. For this reason, perhaps, the average age of dressage riders and horses tends to be a bit higher than in other equestrian sports. It takes a certain amount of youthful derring-do and endurance to compete at eventing and jumping, but dressage requires a control and precision that is not necessarily the forte of young riders and horses— nor even of much interest to them when there are fences to be jumped!

Dressage horses need to be balanced and good natural movers with regular, precise and brilliant gaits. The high-level dressage horse needs also to be something of a show-off, for dressage is a performance sport and requires a horse who is a little vain and fond of attention. Lastly, but of course most importantly, the dressage prospect must be as sound as possible since dressage makes demands on a horse's body, especially the back, neck and hocks. A high proportion of the horses seen in the dressage arena today are German, Dutch and Scandinavian warmbloods. These are large, powerful horses descended from heavy coaching and draft breeds, made lighter and keener by the introduction of Thoroughbred blood. While some say that warmbloods are a fad of the moment and not inherently any more fit for dressage than many other breeds, those who work with them attest to their extraordinary natural balance, carriage and impulsion. Certainly many of the world's top competitors are warmbloods. However, at the lower levels many excellent Thoroughbreds, Quarter Horses and a surprising number of Appaloosas do very well.

Although dressage has always had a following among serious horse people—particularly in Northern Europe—it hasn't become a popular spectator sport until quite recently. The surge in interest is generally attributed to the popularity of the musical ride called the Kur. If other dressage tests can be likened to the compulsories in figure skating, the Kur is like freestyle competition. When the music is well chosen and horse and rider are competent, to watch a Kur is really to watch a dancing horse; the sight is spectacularly beautiful.

COMBINED TRAINING

Combined training, or three-day eventing as it is also known, is three sports combined into one competition. It was originally called "the Military" and was designed as a test of cavalry horses. Although the 1912 Olympics had a three-day event, only cavalry officers competed; the first civilian competitions were not held until the 1950's. One of the great early civilian riders was an American, Michael Page, who won the individual gold medal at the 1963 Olympics in São Paulo, Brazil, aboard Grasshopper, an extraordinarily talented Connemara pony.

The sport underwent some changes at first, but nowadays it consists of three tests. The first is the dressage test. This is a programed ride that the rider has memorized. All horses competing at a given level will do the same test. It is ridden in an arena of a set size which is marked by letters at regular intervals around the ring. These letters and their placement are always the same. Unlike the tests in dressage competitions, the dressage called for in eventing is rather basic, even at the higher levels. Eventing dressage is much closer to the original meaning of the word, which is essentially teaching the horse to carry himself lightly, energetically and in balance at all the gaits. Dressage in this sense ideally should be part of the training of every horse in all disciplines. Today, with the plethora of short-cut training devices and the demand for instant results, such work does not go into most horses. Even at the highest levels of competition, eventing dressage does not include advanced movements like piaffe and passage, pirouettes and flying changes of lead at every step, which are called for in the higher levels of dressage competitions. The eventing test calls for a horse to perform at all three gaits on circles and straight lines. Depending upon the level, more advanced work such as half-pass, shoulder-in and turn on the haunches may also be called for.

The second part of the event is endurance. At full three-day events, this consists of four phases. Phases A and C, roads and tracks, are ridden at a trot and slow canter. At the highest three-day-event level, these two phases total about fifteen miles! Phase B is a steeplechase over seven to nine brush fences, and Phase D is the cross-country phase that most people think of when they think of eventing. This test requires fifteen to twenty-two jumping efforts over a cross-country course that includes ditches, banks, drops, water jumps—obstacles that might be encountered on an actual cross-country ride. Today's course designers are often more imaginative than their predecessors in that they use local themes to lend interest to the jumps. Who could forget the Western saloon jump that competitors were faced with at the Los Angeles Olympics? Unlike show jumping fences, cross-country obstacles are solid and are not constructed to fall down if the horse hits them. Mistakes over such fences frequently result in falls by horse and rider. Riders are given ample opportunity to walk the course on foot beginning on the day before the competition, but the horses (unless they happen to live at the farm where the event is being held) are not schooled over the fences.

The last test is stadium jumping, which takes place over a moderate-sized show jumping course. The idea here is not to see how high the horse can jump but rather as the F.E.I. (Fédération Equestre Internationale, the international governing body of equestrian competition) rules state: "Its sole object is to prove that, on the day after a severe test of endurance, the horses have retained the suppleness, energy and obedience necessary for them to continue in service."

The challenges in eventing are several. First, the requirements for each test are very different, even contradictory. To get a good score in dressage, the horse must be obedient and totally accurate, and carry his body in a shortened frame with his hindquarters more underneath his body than in the relaxed state, and his head and neck more flexed. On cross-country, on the other hand, the horse needs above all to be fit and bold and to be able to think for himself rather than be unswervingly obedient to his rider. Instead of going in a shortened frame, he needs to be able to stretch out to a long, galloping stride to take him from fence to fence and then to be able to shorten or lengthen his stride as needed to get over what sometimes can be rather strange obstacles. In addition, the sort of horse able to do this may be unable to summon the concentration and the obedience necessary to do well in dressage and the fitter the horse, the more likely he is to be full of himself and difficult to ride quietly and accurately in the dressage arena. One plus is that dressage training is the best possible foundation for jumpers. A horse that knows how to carry himself in balance and to change the length of his stride easily is much handier over fences—both over the cross-country fences, which require a bold approach, and over the stadium courses, which may require the horse to make sharp turns and changes of direction and to be a very clever jumper.

Eventing has surged in popularity in the United States over the past twenty years. It is also extremely popular in Great Britain, Ireland, many European countries and Japan. Several excellent international competitors come from Bermuda and Jamaica. Sadly, just as eventing is becoming a popular sport, the open lands needed for holding an event are dwindling. Several events have been ended because of this and the remaining ones tend to be extremely crowded in many parts of the country, with waiting lists for those wishing to compete.

As in show jumping, the sport has an entry level. These competitions are known as horse trials and combined tests. Horse trials are like scaled-down three-day events in that they often take place over one or two rather than three days. Even if a horse trial takes place over three days, the endurance test is considerably shortened. Rather than comprising four phases, there is only the cross-country ride with speed, distance and number of jumping efforts variable according to the level of competition. Combined tests consist of only dressage and stadium jumping.

In ascending order of difficulty, the levels are novice, training, preliminary, intermediate and advanced. Horse trials and combined tests are held at each level. Two- and three-day events begin at the preliminary level which, in spite of its name, are actually quite demanding, marking the boundary line between the lower levels, which act as an introduction to the sport, and the advanced levels, which require an extraordinary high level of fitness and competence on the part of both horse and rider.

One of the most important reasons for the popularity of eventing today is certainly the Pony Club, an organization started in Great Britain in 1928 and in the United States in 1954. Its objective was to provide sound instruction in riding and horse management for children, particularly those who could not otherwise afford it. This organization is responsible for the well-rounded equestrian and stable management education of over one hundred thousand children in twenty-five countries around the world. Many of today's best event riders, particularly among the younger generation, got their first taste of the sport in Pony Club competitions.

POLO

Polo is the most ancient stick-and-ball sport as well as one of the most ancient, and arguably most exciting, equestrian sports. The name derives from the Tibetan *pulu*, which means "willow root," the material the polo ball was originally made from. It is difficult to tell where polo originated. One of the earliest references to it is made in connection with Darius, King of Persia.

It then probably spread to Constantinople and eventually to China and Japan. Invaders brought the game to India, where it was discovered by British planters and cavalry officers during the mid-nineteenth century. In 1859, the British organized the first polo club at Silchar, near Manipur, and drew up the rules of the game. The present-day rules, although based on these, have been modified over the years. The original teams were mounted on small, native Manipuri ponies about 12 hands high and played nine men to a team. By the turn of the century, the height limit had risen to 14.2 hands, the borderline between pony and horse. By 1919, the height requirements were eliminated, and today ponies as big as 16 or more hands are playing successfully. As the ponies became larger, the teams became smaller, finally dropping to the present-day four (three in indoor polo). The first polo match on British soil was played between two British cavalry regiment teams of eight riders each in 1869. This resulted in the founding of the Hurlingham Club, which was to remain the headquarters of British polo until after World War II, when escalating real estate costs and population pressures caused polo to die out in London. Polo also spread throughout the British Empire and to Ireland, the United States and Argentina.

Polo is not unlike hockey on horseback, with the object being to score goals by hitting the ball through goal posts at either end of the 300-yard-long field. This is done by means of a mallet, a bamboo stick bearing a wooden head, angled so that it lies flat on the ground during a shot. The game is divided into periods of seven and a half minutes called chukkers, with rest periods in between. Most games have four chukkers, but large international matches have six or eight.

Polo caught on quickly in North America and if anything is continuing to grow in popularity. It was introduced into the United States in 1876 by James Gordon Bennett, a rich sporting man and newspaper owner. Bennett and some of his wealthy friends founded the Westchester Polo Club in Newport, Rhode Island, the American equivalent of the Hurlingham Club. By 1885 polo was a sport at Harvard, and it soon spread to other universities. Yale and the University of Virginia have figured prominently in college polo.

One of the most important innovations brought to the game by the Americans was the handicapping system for players that was introduced in 1888 by H.L. Herbert. Up to that time, novice players were dominated by much more experienced players. Under the handicapping system, a player is assigned a rating corresponding to the number of goals he might be expected to score in a game (ratings can vary from country to country). The handicap totals of both teams' players are either matched or added, with the lower-rated team receiving the difference. Handicaps range from -1 (-2 in England) to 10. The ratings are adjusted each year by committee.

Although many people tend to think of polo

as a rich man's sport—and certainly the names of many famous players of the past lend support to that contention—early American polo wasn't all the Meadow Brook Club and scions of great fortunes and old families. Polo also became popular early on in California and in Texas, where it was played in cowboy clothes on Western saddles. Texas Quarter Horses and even mustang-type polo ponies became extremely desirable back East. Later on, an ex-cowboy named Cecil Smith was to make polo history by maintaining his 10-goal rating over twenty-five years. Although polo is once again popular—with movie stars, business tycoons, royalty and corporate sponsors—there has been a parallel increase in small local clubs whose members (an increasing number of whom are women) enjoy one or two low-key games a week on the best horses they can find.

Any polo player will tell you that the pony is the most important element in the game. In a high-goal game a player may ride six or more ponies, depending upon the number of chukkers. These ponies must be fast, fit and handy. They must be able to turn on a dime, do flying changes of lead and sliding stops and neck rein. Dressage, while not commonly used in the training of polo ponies, can be extremely helpful in enabling them to do these things without hurting themselves. Although there tends to be a fairly high level of injury to the ponies during games, some ponies nevertheless seem to enjoy the game and know what is expected of them. Experienced ponies are worth many thousands of dollars and are hard to come by. While the average player is likely to ride a Thoroughbred with some Quarter Horse blood, top international players usually ride Argentinian Thoroughbreds.

RODEO

The word *rodeo* means "round-up" in Spanish and rodeo events are cowboy competitions that have their origins in the handling of cattle. Rodeo began as informal competitions between cowboys with time on their hands either after the cattle they had driven to the train junction were loaded or while waiting for the boxcars to arrive. The early contests were simply challenges to demonstrate their superior skills in roping and riding. They took place in the dusty main streets or the stockyards of cow towns. The idea soon spread and more organized competitions were held. In 1883, a public steer-roping contest was held and prize money given to the winner. The Pendleton Roundup in Pendleton, Oregon, which was going strong by the beginning of this century, still continues today. Rodeo eventually became an organized sport with its own professional association. Competitors began to be looked upon as skilled athletes. The best are stars who earn a good living on the circuit.

Most of the five standard rodeo events have their origins in ranch work. *Calf roping* was necessary to catch and tie calves to prepare them for branding or vetting. In today's competitions, the calf is released from the chute a few seconds ahead of the horse and rider. The competitor lassoes the calf, and the horse slides to a stop. The rider secures the other end of the rope to the horn of his saddle and runs toward the calf. This event requires a well-trained horse who understands that his business is to keep the rope taut, thereby keeping the calf on the line. When the competitor reaches the calf, he throws it to the ground on its side and quickly ties its legs with a short "piggin' string." He then must remount and ride toward the calf to slacken the line. The calf must remain tied for six seconds. The best time wins. Champion calf ropers can get the job done in just under ten seconds. Team roping is a similar contest in which two contestants work to rope the calf—one roping the horns and throwing the calf and the other roping its hind feet. Team roping is a recent event that is beginning to become a standard rodeo fixture.

Saddle bronc riding is another vestigial cowboy skill. In the old days, there was no time to train cow ponies. Instead, a semi-wild horse was quickly broken by suddenly being roped and having a saddle thrown across its back. A cowboy with a good seat then climbed aboard and held on until the exhausted horse was all out of bucks.

The same strong seat and good balance are needed in the modern contest. The horse is restrained in a chute. The cowboy lowers himself into a modified stock saddle—one without a horn—and takes hold of the single rope rein attached to the horse's halter. The rider's other hand must not touch the saddle or rein. The horse's natural tendency to buck off such an encumbrance is encouraged by means of a bucking strap tightened around his sensitive loins. The chute opens and the rider must begin spurring the horse as soon as he touches the ground. If the rider fails to spur his horse he will be eliminated. The more he spurs him, his legs swinging wildly, the better his score. The score is based on both the horse's bucking and the rider's performance. The rider must stay on eight seconds.

Bareback riding, although it requires the same sort of skills (except that the horse is bareback), is a much newer sport, having been made an official event in the 1950's. The bareback bronc rider must possess extraordinary balance, agility and strength because all he has to hold on to is a leather strap with a stiff handle on top.

The horses for bucking contests are usually supplied by contractors. Good bucking horses are extremely valuable. While some are merely spoiled or badly broken (or just have sore backs), others are specially bred from good bucking lines. Horses used for calf roping, on the other hand, tend to be ridden by their owners who often put as many years into training their equine partners as the most exacting dressage trainers.

Two standard rodeo events involve steers and are thus immediately much more dangerous.

Steer wrestling, or bull-dogging, begins much like a calf-roping contest, except that the steer is full-grown. Once it is released from the chute, the contestant gallops after it. A "hazer" galloping along the steer's other flank keeps it running in a straight line. When the contestant pulls alongside the running steer, he leans precariously from the saddle to grab the steer by the horns. He then makes a flying dismount, digs his heels into the ground for support and throws the steer to the ground on its side by twisting its neck. The winner is the man with the best time. Although steer wrestling is included among the standard rodeo events, it did not evolve from ranch work and serves no utilitarian purpose. Although the hazer does not compete, his skills and aid are essential to the success and safety of the bull-dogger, as is a quick and unflappable horse for both the bull-dogger and the hazer.

The *bull riding* event is so dangerous that it is almost frightening to watch. Not only do full-grown bulls weigh about a ton, but they are also extremely ferocious when provoked and will charge and gore a downed competitor. For this reason, courageous rodeo clowns and mounted pick-up men are at the ready to distract the angry bull until a fallen cowboy can get up or be moved to safety. Otherwise, the contest is conducted much as other rodeo events, with the bull and rider released from a chute. In this event, however, riders are allowed to hold on with both hands! Riders who dare spur their bulls or who manage to maintain an upright seat are given extra points. Competitors must stay on eight seconds. At the end of the go-round, the mounted pick-up men help the rider to dismount.

Cutting and *reining* contests require completely different skills. Rather than physical prowess, finesse and rapport between horse and rider are the order of the day. Although some rodeos feature cutting contests, there are also separate competitions. Cutting skills are required on the ranch to separate (cut) calves from the herd for breeding or other reasons. Cutting as a sport has many ardent devotees who have never done a day of ranch work in their lives. Cutting is also popular in Australia, South America and other places where there are large cattle ranches.

While other equestrian sports depend upon teamwork, however subtle, between horse and rider, cutting horses work free from interference by their riders, at least in the arena. In fact, the rider is penalized for appearing to cue the horse. The intelligence, balance and, above all, the concentration evident in every sinew of these horses' bodies is something to see. Such performances require a high level of skilled training, which may take several years to sharpen to top competitive level. At the very top, cutting horse competitions offer some of the biggest prize money of any equine event and high-level cutting horses are extremely valuable.

In a cutting contest, a herd of calves is driven into the ring. The horse and rider approach the herd and the rider picks out the calf that will best show off the horse's skills. (Since part of the score is determined by the challenge offered by the calf chosen, this is one of the few ways in which the rider can really influence the result once the horse has entered the ring.) Once the rider has indicated to the horse which calf he wants to cut, the horse goes to work very much like a sheep dog, gently nudging the calf out of the herd and into the center of the arena. (In fact, there are those who feel that the ability that certain breeds such as Quarter Horses, mustangs and Appaloosas have for cutting work is the result of instincts acquired after so many generations of ranch work.) The contestant has two and a half minutes to work, usually time to cut several calves. The score is based on the challenges posed by the calves, the horse's abilities and reactions and any mistakes made by horse or rider.

Reining is the dressage of Western riding and can be as beautiful to watch if not quite as elegant. Reining competitions are designed to show the horse's training and his obedience to his rider in performing a programed ride consisting of movements derived from the requirements of ranch work. These include spins, rollbacks, sliding stops, rein-back and changes of lead. They are done on figure eights, circles and straight lines. Five judges evaluate the performance for accuracy and obedience as well as for smoothness and finesse.

COMBINED DRIVING

Combined driving is one of the newest equestrian sports. While driving and coaching competitions are much older, the pre-1969 driving competitions were generally judged either on turn-out alone or were long-distance races. The organized sport of combined driving dates back to 1964 when it was suggested to the Duke of Edinburgh, then president of the F.E.I., that international rules should be drafted for driving competitions. Competitions for four-in-hand teams with dressage and cross-country tests were already popular in Germany and Hungary, but the rules for international competitors varied from country to country. Even today, under international rules, there are still variations in harnesses, carriages, how the reins are held and how driver, whips and grooms are dressed.

Combined driving competitions comprise Competition A, which includes presentation—where turn-out, condition and grooming are judged—and dressage. The dressage competition is a test of precision in the performance of the figures as well as the style of the driver and the performance of the horses. The dressage tests call for the walk and the working, collected and extended trots. The movements consist of circles and serpentines as well as straight lines. The horses must also demonstrate the halt and rein-back.

Competition B, the marathon, is the most important part of the competition. It is the equivalent of the endurance test of a combined training event and like it is divided into sections. Sections A and C are done at the trot and fast trot, with the former covering nine miles and the latter covering three miles. Sections B and D are done at the walk and are just under a mile each. There are two ten-minute pauses after sections B and D for vet checks and to rest the horses. Section E is done at the trot and is approximately six miles. Along the way, the driver (and the two driving grooms who are in attendance for all three competitions) must negotiate seven or eight hazards. The equivalent of tricky cross-country fences, the hazards may require hairpin turns or the negotiation of steep hills, water or other complications.

In Competition C, obstacle driving, the teams must negotiate a course of up to twenty cones, set only slightly wider than the wheel track of the carriage. As in eventing, the drivers may walk both the marathon and the obstacle courses prior to attempting them.

Penalties are incurred for infractions in each of the competitions, but the rules call for the relative values of competitions as follows: 0.5 presentation, 3 dressage, 10 marathon and 1 obstacle.

Even though it is probably the most expensive, and one of the most time-consuming, of the equestrian sports, combined driving has an increasing number of local and international competitions. It is also popular among spectators for its elegance and sheer beauty as well as its excitement.

HORSE RACING

Flat racing is the province of the Thoroughbred, a breed developed in England at the end of the seventeenth century and the beginning of the eighteenth century. All Thoroughbreds trace back to one of three foundation sires: the Godolphin Arabian, the Byerly Turk and the Darley Arabian.

Some Thoroughbreds are started at two years of age in the United States, usually over short distances like five furlongs. But the most important flat races in America are those for three-year-olds, and those comprising the Triple Crown are perhaps the most famous: the Kentucky Derby, run at Churchill Downs on the first Saturday in May; the Preakness Stakes, run two weeks later at Pimlico; and the Belmont Stakes, run at Belmont Park, three weeks after that. The Triple Crown has been won only eleven times since 1919, although many horses have won two of the races. The Derby and the Preakness are both a mile and a quarter while the Belmont is a mile and a half. Although open to both colts and fillies, very few fillies are ever entered. Fillies have their own Triple Crown: the Kentucky Oaks, the Coaching Club American Oaks and the Mother Goose Stakes.

The British Triple Crown consists of the 2,000 Guineas, run at Newmarket; the Derby, run at Epsom Downs; and the St. Leger, run at Doncaster and open to both colts and fillies. The distances range from one mile to a mile and three-quarters. Not many horses have won the Triple Crown—the most recent being the dazzling Nijinsky in 1970.

One of the most spectacular American Triple Crown winners was Secretariat. Those who saw Secretariat win the Belmont in 1973, thereby clinching the first Triple Crown in a quarter of a century, will never forget the utter splendor of that bright chestnut colt as he pulled away from the pack and drove on with such raw power that the other horses appeared to be standing still! He won the race by 31 lengths and set a new track record, as he did in each of the other two Triple Crown races.

Another big chestnut horse captured the hearts of Americans and made his name synonymous with horse racing. He was Man O'War, owned by Samuel Riddle. Bought for $5,000 at the 1918 Saratoga yearling sales, he won a total of $249,465 and was beaten only once in twenty-one starts. His one defeat is usually attributed to jockey error since his rider that day, Johnny Loftus, managed to let him get boxed in on the rail and unable to make a move. When he finally did get free, he ran for all he was worth to catch up but lost the race by only half a length. Although he did not run in the Kentucky Derby, he won the other legs of the Triple Crown. Man O'War died in 1947, and not long afterward so did his adoring groom, Will Harbutt, who had proclaimed his charge "the mostest horse that ever was."

Steeplechasing originated in Ireland and England during the eighteenth century with fox hunters who enjoyed jumping the higher obstacles and fences that the Enclosure Acts caused to be constructed.

In Ireland and in England, where there are many specialized tracks for the sport, steeplechasing is a race over jumps which can be hurdles, brush or timber. Hurdle races take place over fences made of brush and rails that incline about sixty degrees in the direction the horse is moving. Young steeplechasers—three- or four-year-olds—often begin their steeplechasing careers over hurdles and may race over them one or two seasons before going on. Brush races are run over a course that includes ditches and a water jump as well as fences that look like enormous hedges. Some of the courses have unique fences, such as the Irish Banks at Punchestown in Ireland or Becher's Brook at Aintree in England. Timber races or point-to-points are often put on by hunts and usually take place over high post-and-rail fences, which require accurate jumping as they tend to be quite solid—unlike hurdles or brush which can be grazed by the horse's feet with impunity.

The famous races in England are the Grand National and the Cheltenham Gold Cup. In Ireland, it's the Leopardstown Chase and the Irish Sweeps Derby. In the United States, the important steeplechases are the Grand National, the Temple Gwathmey and the Colonial Cup.

Many of the most renowned jump racers have been English or Irish horses. Perhaps the most famous of the latter was an Irish-bred bay named Red Rum. "Rummie" was reincarnated by a knowledgeable trainer from a first life of races lost to chronic lameness to run the Aintree Grand National five times, winning it three times and finishing second twice. His last win, in 1977 when he was twelve, set a record that is still unbroken. His career ended on the eve of his sixth Grand National when he was injured and had to be scratched. Although Red Rum was originally bought as a yearling for about 500 dollars, he was the top-earning jump racer of his time.

Another great Irish horse was the big bay Arkle, who was defeated only four times out of thirty-two steeplechases. Two of these defeats were attributed to his being overburdened by the handicapper, one to a slip and the last to the fracture that ended his illustrious career.

More popular than brush and hurdle races in the United States are timber races, or point-to-points, in which both professionals and amateurs compete and horses do not have to be registered Thoroughbreds. The most important timber race is the Maryland Hunt Cup, but many others are held in Pennsylvania, Maryland, Virginia and the Carolinas, where there are still many active hunts. The sport is increasing in popularity in the Midwest and there are several point-to-points in Colorado and California. The point-to point scene is much more informal than other types of American steeplechasing with families and friends enjoying plenty of gossip and tail-gate picnics.

FOX HUNTING

Hunting from horseback is one of man's earliest uses of the horse. Hunting was first a way of getting food and later a way of killing predators that stole livestock. Many of the early packs were organized by large landholders or by groups of farmers. Today hunting still survives, but only as a sport. The fox is the most common quarry of mounted hunters throughout the world, although in elite European circles deer, stag and wild boar are hunted. In the western United States, coyote and hare are frequently hunted.

Hunting embodies a pageantry and a protocol that are rare in modern life. The dress code is strict and meaningful. The red jackets that most people associate with hunts are worn only by seasoned gentlemen members of the field. Everyone else wears black. The black velvet-covered helmets that are always worn in horse shows are worn only by the Master of Foxhounds (MFH) and the hunt staff and children. Others must wear less safe black bowlers. Distinguished members of the field are awarded the hunt's colors to wear on their collar and buttons with the hunt's insignia. Protocol also dictates where in the field a rider stays. Seasoned hunt members and guests invited to so do by the MFH hunt up front, just behind the master. Children, the elderly and those on green horses and kickers bring up the rear. It is definitely frowned upon to ride out of place, and riders with uncontrollable green horses who gallop past the field and end up behind the master are asked not to bring them back!

Any horse that is sound and sane and a good jumper can be used for hunting. Of paramount importance is good manners around the hounds and other horses. Horses that may be brilliant show hunters over a course of fences in a ring may be impossible to control in the field. The most renowned hunters, prized throughout the hunting world and widely exported, are those bred in Ireland from Irish draft and Thoroughbred stock. They are usually quite heavy, with plenty of bone and an unflappable disposition. There is nothing quite like the feeling of riding one of these big safe horses who has learned to handle himself over the rugged terrain and truly fearsome fences encountered out hunting in many parts of Ireland.

Hunting depends upon well-trained foxhounds, which are always called hounds, never dogs. They are purebred American or English foxhounds and are under the control of the huntsman, often a professional who is in charge of the kennels and breeding. Hound shows are another important aspect of the hunting world.

Although some consider fox hunting a barbaric sport, few foxes are killed nowadays. There are those who say that the wily creatures actually enjoy confusing the hounds and giving them a good run before going safely to ground. More and more common are drag hunts, in which the hounds follow an artificial fox scent dragged over a set course.

Anyone who has ever witnessed a hunt meet assembling at dawn on a day in autumn will never forget the gloriousness of the spectacle, a vanishing way of life as more and more of the countryside becomes commercially developed and closed to horses and hounds.

IN CONCLUSION

The horse is many things to many people. For some, it is a means of livelihood; for others it is a companion in sport or on a relaxed trail ride. For still others, it is a symbol of power and beauty that they never grow tired of watching and never fail to appreciate, whether it's a mustang running wild, a Thoroughbred at a morning workout at Saratoga, a carriage horse on the streets of Vienna, a mare and foal in a Kentucky pasture, or a backyard pony anywhere. It is hoped that what the horse embodies for so many, has been captured even in some small degree.

Facing page: A beautifully marked Palomino stallion. The Palomino is only recognized as a breed in some countries, others preferring to label it as a color. Top: A pair of Münsterland heavy horses, displaying the variation of color typical of the breed. Such heavy horses were used extensively for farm work in Germany until the internal combustion engine replaced them as the main source of power earlier this century. Above: A fine portrait of an Andalusian horse. Andalusia was that part of Spain conquered by the Moors in the 8th century and the Andalusian horse derives from a cross between the native Spanish horses and the fine Arabs brought in by the newcomers.

Top: A pair of Falabella ponies almost dwarfed by the daffodils among which they are grazing. The breed was developed in Argentina and, at only two feet tall, is the smallest in the world. Unlike other breeds the Falabella is completely useless and is only kept as a show pony. Above: A French Saddle mare follows her foal to water. Facing page top: A group of Arabs, grazing on lush pasture.

Facing page bottom: A herd of shaggy Exmoor ponies on the sparse grasslands of their native highlands. The Exmoor is considered to be directly descended from the ancient Celtic Pony of northwestern Europe and retains many features bred out of more recent lines of horses.

Above: A Hafflinger mare, the modern, formalized form of the native Tyrol mountain pony. Until 1873 there was no recognized breed of pony in the area, but the introduction of a fine Arab stallion and the inauguration of breeding records led to the establishment of this popular type. Facing page: the shaggy head of a Welsh Mountain Pony. Like the Hafflinger the Welsh Pony derives from a cross between native ponies and Arabs and has become much used as a children's pony.

Generally considered to be the finest horse breed in the world, the Arab (top and facing page) has a long, but obscure history. According to legend all modern Arabs are descended from the horses owned by the prophet Mohammed, the founder of Islam, in the 6th century. However archaeologists have found paintings dating back more than two thousand years earlier which show nearly identical horses belonging to the Pharaohs of Egypt. The Lipizzaner (above), by contrast has well-known origins. Charles, Archduke of Austria, established the breed in 1580 with horses imported from Spain, though later native German horses were added to the stock.

Above: When confronted by an unusual or interesting smell horses will adopt this expression, known as the flehmen. By curling its lips and depressing the nostrils, the horse is able to gain a fuller appreciation of the scent. Facing page: A portrait of an Arab stallion. The Arab originated as the work horse of the nomadic tribesmen of the Nejd. The tribesmen demanded stamina, strength and courage in their horses and ruthlessly weeded out any animal which failed to display these qualities. Arabs, and Arab-crosses, are now bred in many countries, but the nomads continue to raise the horses with a pride undiminished by the centuries.

The English Thoroughbred (these pages and overleaf) is often considered to be the finest racing horse and is seen on race tracks throughout the world. It derives from an 18th century cross between native British running horses and Arab stallions. All modern Thoroughbreds must be able to show their ancestry back to one of three stallions to qualify for the breed, though most descend from all three. Above: Exercising on the Lambourn Downs. Top: Racing at Cheltenham. Facing page top: Contestants in the Hereford Point-to-Point clear a fence. Facing page bottom: Entrants in a race at Cheltenham circling the paddock.

The sport of horse racing must be as old as horse-riding itself for owners have always wished to test the skill and stamina of their mounts. It is known that the Ancient Olympic Games featured horse races as early as 624 BC and that the Pharaohs of Egypt raced their mounts. However, the modern sport developed during the 17th century in England as noblemen matched their horses against each other. Formalized rules gradually took shape and in 1751 the Jockey Club was formed to organize the sport. Racing around the world now follows similar rules: (facing page) in the USA; (top) in Czechoslovakia and (above) in Britain.

The British Royal Family has been closely associated with horse racing for many generations. Charles II, who ruled in the late 17th century, was particularly fond of the sport, and acted as supreme judge in all disputes between owners. The traditional link continues to our own day with Royal Ascot (facing page) being a major ceremonial occasion which opens with the Royal carriages parading along the course. Several other British meetings, such as Epsom (this page), where the Derby is run, are equally grand and have their own ceremonies and dress regulations.

Most horse breeds produced in a specific region are bred to suit the purpose for which they shall be used, a feature clearly seen in the north German breeds of Holstein and Oldenburg. The Oldenburg (top) was first produced during the 17th century as a large horse suitable for both farm and military work. During peacetime it was used on the land, but during wartime was used to pull artillery. It needed to combine the stamina required for the farm with the spirit used in war, a combination it still exhibits. The Holstein (above) is a powerfully built riding horse, popular in jumping competitions. Facing page top: A trio of Portuguese horses.

The French River Rhone enters the Mediterranean through a large delta which covers hundreds of square miles. In this marshy wilderness live the wild herds of Camargue Ponies (these pages and overleaf) which have made the region famous. The horses have an ancient ancestry which may be traced back to the original wild horses of France, but interbreeding with domestic horses has affected their appearance. The 30 or so herds live wild, though they are sometimes rounded up and prospective mounts captured. These greys are difficult to handle as mounts, but are agile and nimble when properly trained.

Over a thousand years of isolation have produced the Icelandic Pony (top). This hardy breed originated with the small ponies brought to Iceland by the Vikings who settled this remote island around the year AD 900. The importation of fresh horses was later banned because of fear of disease so the breed has bred true for centuries. The ponies are rarely over 13 hands tall and have long been used both as mounts and as pack animals. Much of the rugged, roadless interior of the island remains accessible only by pony. Facing page: A small child's pony in New Jersey. Above: A semi-wild horse searches for food among the winter snows of Wyoming.

Though similar in coloring, the Hafflinger (above and top) and the Palomino (facing page) are quite different animals. The Hafflinger is a recognized breed of pony which is popular in its native Austria and whose breeding is regulated by a national body. The Palomino, however, is merely a color, which can be produced in several breeds.

The chestnut coat and white mane and tail are the product of crossing a cream horse with a chestnut. If two palominos are crossed their offspring have only a 50/50 chance of being palomino, others revert to cream or chestnut. It is the ability to breed pure which distinguishes a breed from a color or cross.

The various types of Welsh Pony (these pages) are all derived from the Welsh Mountain Pony which has lived in those highlands for over 2,000 years. The original animal was a fast, sure-footed animal employed for cattle herding and for warfare, and much used for crossing with other breeds. More recently the introduction of Arab blood has produced larger and more graceful animals, though some claim that the breed has lost something of its character. The Holstein (overleaf) has also changed recently. Long famous as big riding horses, which also took well to harness, the Holstein has recently been bred smaller and lighter as the demand for carriage work has declined.

The modern sport of show-jumping had its origins in the hunting field with participants rather than spectators. In the course of fox-hunting riders and horses needed to cope with a variety of obstacles, ranging from gates and hedges to streams and ponds. Contests between riders at clearing difficult local obstacles gradually became formalized into show-jumping, as we know it, between 1860, when the first local event was run in Ireland, and 1900, when the first international contest was held. Facing page: Robert Ehrenz on Koh-i-nor. Above left: Michael Whitaker on Warren Point. Above right: John Whitaker on Next Milton. Top: Ulrich Meyer on Merano.

Show-jumping is arranged as both an indoor and an outdoor event, and the two differ considerably. Indoor events tend to have short courses and a limited number of fences while outdoor courses are longer and have a greater variety of obstacles. The bank (above left) is a common outdoor fence, demanding skill and timing from both the rider and the horse. Rail fences can be easily constructed and removed, so forming the most variable and demanding part of any course. Facing page: Harvey Smith on Shining Example. Top: B. Langram on Grey Twist. Above left: Peter Charles on April Sun. Above right: Conrad Hornfeld on Abdullah.

The skills demanded of horses and riders during three day events and show-jumping were first perfected by the military. The cavalry of the 19th century were expected to master a wide range of skills, such as scouting ahead of the infantry, long range raiding into enemy territory and charging enemy troops. All these demanded not only discipline, but also the ability to negotiate any obstacle which the terrain, or enemy, might place in the way. Cavalry men and mounts were put through rigorous training, including cross-country races and obstacle courses. The military still feature highly in eventing, although few cavalry regiments still ride horses to war. Above: Mario Deslouriers on Box Car Willie. Facing page top: An amateur rider at a local British event in Bath. Facing page bottom: John Ledingham on Kilcorltrim.

Both the ancient and modern Olympic Games feature equestrian events, though both lacked them for the first few meetings. The competitions were, however, quite different. The modern events include dressage, show-jumping and three day eventing, for both teams and individuals. The ancient games featured only two individual contests. The first was a straight bareback horse race on a track about) mile long, but the more popular was a chariot race around an oval course. Sometimes as many as 35 chariots with four horses apiece took part, and crashes were so common that rarely more than half finished. The modern sports seem almost tame by comparison. Facing page top: Francois van der Broeck on Wellington. Facing page bottom: The victorious USA team after winning the 1984 Olympic Two Day Event. Above: John Whitaker on Novilheiro.

Show jumping is a specialized form of equestrian sport which demands a special horse, though exactly what this horse should be is hard to define. Traditionally hunters were used for jumping contests, though since 'hunter' was a term used for any horse suitable for hunting this could mean almost anything. Modern jumpers are of similarly mixed stock with Holsteins being popular in Germany while a Thoroughbred/draught cross is favored in Britain. The horse needs to be muscular and have strong joints to absorb the impact of landing. Facing page: Annette Lewes on Tutfin. Above left: Anne Kursinkski on Starman. Above right: Jan van der Schaus on Olympic Trotter. Top: Harvey Smith, one of the best-known British show-jumpers.

The care of horses throughout the year varies greatly from area to area and between owners. Wild horses are able to survive year round in the lands where they live for they have evolved to suit their home. In some areas horses can be left outside year-round, as at Wurtemburg (overleaf), where snows are infrequent. Shetland Ponies (facing page bottom) were bred in the chilly Shetland Islands off Scotland and so can survive most climates. Other horses need more care and spend the winter in stables. In areas where pasture is limited horses may spend many hours each day in their stables, where they can be fed and cared for more easily.

Few truly wild horses remain in the world. The Mongolian Wild Horse, or Przevalski's Horse, is almost extinct in the wild, though several herds are kept in captivity. However, many wilderness areas support herds of domestic horses which have gone wild, and now live completely natural lives. The Mustangs of the American West (above) are derived from the horses of the Spanish Conquistadores which were of crossed-Arab stock. Their tough life has led to a diminution in size. The Brumbies of Australia (facing page top) are larger, but even more cunning and shy. One of the classics of Australian literature, *The Man from Snowy River*, concerns a herd of Brumbies. Top: An English horse at pasture. Facing page bottom: Horses in Colorado.

The Arab (these pages) is easily the most important horse used in crossing, and has been used to improve many local breeds around the world. The breed originated in the deserts of Arabia, where it was used as a war horse by the tribes who lived by raiding trade caravans and each other. The tribesmen were ruthless owners, who kept only the finest horses for stud purposes. The superb qualities of the breed were preserved by such methods, but modern breeders outside Arabia have often been accused of being increasingly concerned with producing large numbers of foals for sale, rather than maintaining standards. The Welsh Pony (overleaf) is a noted result of crossing Arabs with native stock.

The sport of foxhunting from horseback is an established part of British life, and has been introduced to areas, such as New England and Australia, where large numbers of English families have settled. The modern form of hunting came into being about 250 years ago when a variety of factors produced suitable conditions. The clearance of wide areas of forest produced open country ideal for hunting on horseback. At the same time the extermination of wild boar and deer made fox the only wild animal worth hunting to thrive in large numbers. The introduction of the Arab to British horsebreeding produced a fast horse capable of maintaining a high speed for long periods of time, an ideal mount for the chase.

British foxhunting, (facing page and overleaf) the Cotswold Hunt and (top) the Hurlworth Hunt, is organized around a simple pattern common to most hunts. The pack is the responsibility of the Master of Hounds who keeps the pack on the scent of the fox and who controls the field, steering it away from land closed to hunting. The members of the hunt, and visiting riders, follow the course of the hunt, being free to choose their own line over hedges and other obstacles. French hunting, or *Venerie*, (above) Rallye l'Aumonce, is far more complicated. The hunt takes place in dense forest and the hunters keep in touch by means of horn signals. The *Venerie* hunt deer, moving in several groups in order to steer the deer in the desired direction, rather than chasing their quarry as in British fox and hare hunting.

The social side of foxhunting has always been important, but has changed greatly over the years. Originally packs were kept by noblemen for the use of themselves and their friends. By the early 19th century many hunts were being funded by groups of the lesser gentry who divided the cost between them. It was at this time that hunt balls became the great annual social events they have remained, with their own traditions and favored dances. After the Second World War hunting became more broadly based with local farmers riding to hounds alongside landowners and wealthy businessmen. The modern hunt is far more popular and better supported than in previous generations. Facing page top: The Taunton Vale Hunt. Top: The Beaufort Hunt. Above: The Exmoor Hounds. Facing page bottom: Exercising English Thoroughbreds in winter.

Facing page: A Highland Pony, or Garron, from the mountains of northern Scotland. Although today it is a recognized breed, the pony was formerly cross-bred with many other types to produce a practical working horse irrespective of ancestry. Used traditionally as a riding and pack horse by the farmers of the Highlands, the pony was later used by deer stalkers who needed a tough, quiet horse to carry guns and bags through the wild moorlands. Top: A portrait shot of a fine Holstein mare, a noted large riding horse from Germany. Above left: A Münsterland Heavy, much used for farm work. Above right: A wild Camargue Pony from southern France.

Ponies are generally small horses, under 14 hands, which are hardy, stocky and have thick coats. They are usually localized breeds which have developed to suit particular conditions where larger horses are either not needed or would be impracticable. The New Forest Pony (previous pages), of southern England, can be very variable in both size and markings, perhaps due to its mixed ancestry. The Shetland Pony (top) is small, around 40 inches, and used as a packhorse on its native Scottish islands. The Norwegian Fjord Pony (above left) is very docile and is useful for farm work. The Dartmoor Pony (above right), of England, lives wild, with numbers being taken for training each year. The Dülmen Pony (facing page bottom) of Germany likewise live wild, with young horses taken for riding. Facing page top: The Norwegian Wild Pony.

Previous pages: Two magnificently turned out pairs of Shire Horses dragging harrows at an agricultural show in England. Heavy horses were used for agricultural work for centuries, and large farms might have had as many as two dozen animals. The Shire was first bred in the Midlands about two centuries ago and has quite extraordinary strength. Facing page: A young Holstein stallion. Above: The shaggy winter coat of a Wurtemburg mare. The Wurtemburg is a spirited and agile horse which is often used for sports. Overleaf: A magnificent black Morgan, one of the finest all-round work horses in the world.

The Germans have long been enthusiastic breeders of horses, and have produced some of the finest breeds in the world. The Hafflinger (top) is a famous Alpine pony well adapted to steep slopes and sparse pasture. The South German Cold-Blood, or Norika, (above) comes from Bavaria where its strength and reliability made it popular with hill farmers and the army for draught work. Facing page top: A trio of German Thoroughbreds, a breed derived from their British counterparts. Facing page bottom: A striking Trakehner bred in Prussian lands which now form part of Poland. Until the Second World War the Trakehner was the most numerous horse in Germany, being used extensively by the army and Government, but it is now rather rare.

The western plains of North America would have been untamable without the horse. The ranchers and farmers of the last century could not have survived without their horses, a fact well realized in the area. Each year the Canadian city of Calgary organizes a Stampede (these pages) where horsemen match their skills against each other in contests such as chuck-wagon racing (top and facing page bottom), steer-wrestling (facing page top) and lassoing (above). Similarly dependent on their horses were the 19th century Mounties, or Royal Northwest Mounted Police, who kept law and order throughout the vast western lands of Canada. The police maintain a display team to show their horse skills (overleaf)

The Spanish sport of bullfighting is, in Portugal, carried on from horseback and rarely involves the death of the bull. The skill lies in the horseman, or *rejoneador*, bringing his mount as close as possible to the bull and touching it with a pole. The training of a *rejoneador* horse is complicated and precise. Otherwise the rider might find himself at the mercy of the bull. The horse is first taught an elaborate dressage system which will allow it to sidestep the bull's charges. Then it is trained as a herding animal so that it becomes used to the smell and sight of cattle. The horse is then put through its paces against a man equipped with bull's horns and only then will it be allowed to face a bull, whose horns have been cut. The final product is possibly the most highly-trained sport horse in the world.

The British Household Cavalry (these pages) still maintain their horses and cavalry uniform for ceremonial occasions, but fight in tanks and armored cars. In the past, however, the regiments fought on horseback. The role of heavy cavalry such as these was to form massive battering ram formations on the battlefield, smashing their way through enemy lines. To an infantry man a 16 hand horse bearing a six-foot man armed with a sword and approaching at full gallop was a formidable adversary. At the Battle of Waterloo in 1815 the Life Guards, and other heavy cavalry regiments, charged their way through a column of 20,000 French infantry, halting the main French advance in its tracks.

For hundreds of years the cavalry of the British army played a vital role on the battlefield. Today, however, the mounted regiments perform solely ceremonial functions. The Blues and Royals (top and facing page top) form escorts to the Royal family at coronations, weddings and other occasions. At state ceremonies the trumpeters and drum majors wear elaborate costumes, heavy with gold thread and embroidery (facing page bottom). The Kings Troop Royal Horse Artillery (above) fire royal salutes on state occasions and perform display rides. Until the First World War horse artillery played a vital battlefield role, bringing guns up to crisis areas at the gallop.

The epitome of formal horsemanship is to be found in the *haute ecole* of classical dressage. The acknowledged masters of the art are the riders of the Spanish Riding School in Vienna (above right, top and facing page bottom) who train their mounts to rear, kick, trot, walk and sidestep with amazing accuracy. These skills originated on the battlefields of 17th century Europe when cavalry fought at close quarters. It was essential for a rider to be able to move his horse in any direction in order to avoid sword thrusts or bullets. The more dynamic maneuvers of the Kathi Horse (facing page top) originated on later, more free-flowing battlefields. Above left: An Andalusian horse performing dressage.

Horses are to be found all over the globe, both as native breeds and as imports to lands previously lacking in horses. The New Forest Ponies (top) are indigenous to the New Forest of southern England and have evolved to suit the environment. Despite its name the forest contains few trees and is made up mainly of heathlands and moors. The horses run wild and have evolved to suit the landscape. Other English horses (remaining pictures) are cared for and less adapted to the environment. The remote Easter Island in the Pacific had no native horses, but today sizeable herds run the grasslands (overleaf) and are used as transport by the local farmers.

Above: The Norwegian pony has a distinctive dun color and a mane of mixed dun and black hairs. Wild ponies, such as this, have shaggy coats and straggly manes, but domestic varieties are neater and farmers usually trim the manes so that they stand upright. The Noriker (facing page top) of southern Germany are medium-heavy work horses which can trace their ancestry back nearly 2,000 years to the days of the Romans. Facing page bottom: A magnificent black Fell Pony running wild on the hills of the English Lake District.

Above: A small herd of the beautiful Lipizzaner greys, an almost exclusively Austrian breed. The Lipizzaners originated with 33 animals imported from Spain by Archduke Charles of Austria in 1580. The breed takes its name from the stud farm at Lipizza where the horses lived until 1918, when they were moved to Piber. The horses are used by the Spanish Riding School and only those horses which have shown great dressage ability are allowed to breed, numbering no more than 150 at any one time. The Thoroughbred, by contrast, exists in large numbers in many lands, including Hungary (facing page and top) and Australia (overleaf).

French Thoroughbred racing began in the 1690s when French noblemen imported Thoroughbreds from England and organized races between their new purchases. It was not until 1777 that standardized rules came into being on the instructions of King Louis XVI. The greatest modern race is the famous Prix de l'Arc de Triomphe (facing page) which is run at Longchamps, in the Bois de Boulogne near Paris. This course was opened in 1857 when it became clear that Parisians needed a racecourse of their own, rather than travel miles into the country to follow the sport. Above: Mtoto, winner of the 1988 Arc de Triomphe.

Thoroughbred racing in the United States dates back to colonial days when well-to-do English gentry brought their horses over with them and laid out a race track near to New York in the 1660s. Today the sport is centered on the 'bluegrass' region of Kentucky where lush meadows provide rich grazing for the stud farms (facing page bottom) and training centers. Appropriately the greatest American classic, the Kentucky Derby is held at Churchill Downs (above and facing page top) near Louisville, in the heart of the region. The racetrack is one of the best-loved in the nation with its wooden grandstand and old-world charm.

In Britain the sport of Thoroughbred racing is well-established and tightly controlled by the Jockey Club. Meetings, usually lasting three or four days, take place on permanent racecourses and normally include many races for different ages of horse. Previous pages: A large field leaves the starting gates at Kempton. Top: A trio of riders dash for the finish at Sandown Park, Surrey. Above: Horses parade before the public prior to a race at Sandown Park. Facing page top: A large field gallops past the grandstand at York. Facing page bottom: An amateur rider races to victory at a provincial racecourse.

Previous pages: A pair of modern Tarpans. The original Tarpan was the wild horse of central Europe, living in forests and open glades. It was a small horse with a large head and light coloration with a distinctive dark stripe down the center of its back. By the start of the last century the wild herds were extinct, though some Tarpans were kept by Polish peasants. In recent years attempts have been made to recreate the wild Tarpan by breeding out domestic characteristics from the Polish animals, with some success. Top: A fine Holstein. Above: A pair of Camargue Ponies. Facing page top: A grey Thoroughbred. Facing page bottom: A spirited Holstein.

The Lipizzaner is one of the rarest and most distinctive breeds of horse in the world. They are kept almost exclusively by the Spanish Riding School in Austria and rarely number more than 500 individuals. These horses are fairly large, standing 16 hands at the shoulder, and have muscular, but elegant, bodies. They are almost all greys, though young horses may be much darker. Despite the small numbers, and even fewer breeding animals, the breed is prevented from stagnating by the occasional introduction of foreign blood, such as Arabs or German hunters. This maintains the high degree of agility and intelligence for which the breed is noted.

The fashionable Swiss holiday resort of St Moritz is best known for its skiing and toboggan facilities, in particular the famous Cresta Run which winds down the mountain side just outside of town. But the winter sports which attract so many thousands each year are not restricted to skis and sledges. The long lake which lies below the town freezes over in winter, providing a large flat area for equestrian sports. Horse racing (facing page top) is popular, but the more exciting sport of polo (above, top and facing page bottom) demands more skill and daring, particularly on the icy surface of the lake.

Top: A hurdles race held on the frozen lake of St Moritz, Switzerland. Harness racing (above) is often regarded as a sport of the United States, but it takes place in other countries as well, such as England (facing page top). The Standardbred, the breed used for harness racing, has its origins with the Thoroughbred, but has developed along quite different lines which are determined by the need to pull, rather than carry its load. An exciting winter variation of harness racing involves light sleighs racing across frozen lakes, (facing page bottom) in Switzerland. Overleaf: Horses dash for the finish across the ice at St Moritz.

The holiday resort of St Moritz, high in the Swiss Alps is a popular destination both in summer and winter. During the warmer months it serves as a focus for walking and trekking, but during the winter is the site of many exciting snow sports, including a variety of equestrian events. Standard horse races are held around a course built on the frozen lake (facing page top) and trotting races are held in which the horses pull light sledges rather than the standard two-wheeled carts. The most thrilling of all is the strange sport of skijoring (top) in which men on skis are towed around a course by horses.

In the wild, horses live in herds of varying sizes and roam at will over the broad grasslands which are their natural habitat. Usually the herd behaves peacefully, as (facing page bottom) in Montana, but occasionally fights will break out, (above) in Wyoming. Such fights are rare, for differences in social rank are usually achieved by threats and display. When fights do occur, however, they can be extremely violent with the loser sustaining severe injuries from kicks and bites. Top: A mare answers a call from a horse kept in a nearby paddock, such vocal communications form an important part in herd behavior and are rarely absent even in domestic horses (facing page top).

These pages: Hungarian Thoroughbreds at a stud farm. The Magyars, the people of Hungary, have been famous as horsemen from the dawn of their history in the 9th century. Late in that century the Magyars invaded the Danube Basin from southern Russia. They fought as mounted archers, riding small, nimble ponies and preferred raiding to set battles. Hungarian cavalry dominated European warfare again some 800 years later when the Austrian Empire raised several regiments of cavalry scouts, known as hussars, from among the Magyars. The hussars were so successful that most European armies trained a few of their own regiments in hussar tactics. Even today some regiments in the British army are referred to as hussars, although they now use tanks.

The greatest steeplechase race in the world is the British Grand National which is run each year at Liverpool's Aintree course. The first race was run in 1836 when a hotel-owner laid the course out next to his hotel to improve business. The course is notoriously difficult, with large jumps and awkward turns. One of the largest obstacles is The Chair (these pages and overleaf) which is the fifteenth fence and, unlike most others, is only jumped once. It is built of spruce branches and stands over five feet tall, funneling the field into a gap just ten feet wide. The size of the jumps has recently been reduced following the deaths of several horses which fell awkwardly.

Steeplechase racing (these pages) is particularly popular in Britain and Ireland, where it began, but has spread only slowly to other parts of the world. In origin the races were run between two churches with the riders choosing their own line to the distant church steeple, hence the name, jumping whatever obstacles got in their way. The winner of the first recorded steeplechase walked away with a barrel each of wine, rum and port as a prize. The modern sport is run on courses over specially built fences, constructed of brushwood or twigs. Some races, however, are run over more formidable obstacles and a few genuine steeplechases, now termed point-to-point, are still run. Overleaf: Exercising English Thoroughbreds in winter.

Above left: A pair of rugged Icelandic Ponies. These small animals have a phenomenal homing instinct unusual in horses. It was a common custom in the past for Icelandic farmers to borrow a horse from a neighbor to ride to town or to home. The pony only needed to be turned loose to return to its own stable. Above right: A modern Tarpan, a recreation of the now extinct wild Tarpan, scents the air at Popiellno, where two small herds live wild. Top: Portrait of an Arab stallion. Facing page top: Shetland Ponies. Facing page bottom: Australian Ponies, a breed derived from crossbreeding imported British ponies, such as the Shetland and Exmoor.

Facing page: A Dülmen Pony, a rare breed from West Germany which are characteristically dark in color and stand around 12 hands high. Above left: A strongly marked Paint. Horses marked with these irregular patches of color were particularly common among the American Indians, who preferred the broken markings because of their camouflage effect. Seen from a distance the lack of a solid horse-shaped outline makes the horse difficult to notice. Above right: A lone Icelandic Pony regards the photographer warily. Top: A pair of Icelandic Ponies indulging in mutual coat-nibbling. Such behavior is common among wild or nearly wild horses, helping to strengthen relationships within the herd. Overleaf: Horses in Montana.

The Andalusian (facing page and above) is the most famous horse breed of Spain. It is an elegant animal with a naturally high-stepping gait which has made it particularly popular as a riding horse. When walking the Andalusian lifts its forelegs up nearly level with the chest and swings them out as they return to the ground. This showy walk has made it popular as a parade horse and is highly prized by landowners and bullfighters as a complement to their fine fiesta costumes. It therefore commands a correspondingly high price. Top: A Holstein mare.

As with many other equestrian sports, four-in-hand driving developed from an everyday working relationship between man and horse. In this case it was the stage coaches which once linked all the major cities of Europe. The drivers of these vehicles, popularly known as Jehus after the Biblical chariot driver, tried to outdo each other in speed and skill. In time the speed trials along public roads developed into contests of skill. Today the driving competitions are held over specially constructed courses which may be short and intricate, placing emphasis on turning control, or a cross-country route several miles in length.

The sport of carriage driving is not merely concerned with speed or skill at negotiating obstacles, though that plays a part, the appearance of the carriage is of prime importance. In a standard three day event, the judges first inspect the presentation of the horses, carriage, driver and passengers, awarding points out of 50 for style, cleanliness, road-worthiness and a host of other criteria. The ensemble then performs a dressage display, consisting of steps and turns. The second day is taken up by a cross-country drive while the third involves an obstacle course. In recent years the sport has greatly benefited from the active support of Britain's Prince Philip, seen (facing page) driving in the 1985 Windsor event.

When a horse is being shown, either for competition or for sale, it is usually put through its paces before the judges or prospective buyers inspect the animal more closely. The object is to display the elegance of the horse and to prove that it has no limps or tenderness in its limbs. Such displays may be done either from the saddle, as (facing page top) or by leading the horse by a bridle, as (facing page bottom). The magnificent stallion being shown (above) was awarded a premium by the Hunters' Improvement Society, thus gaining recognition as a first class stud animal.

The many differences between wild and domestic horses can be traced to the fact that wild horses are free from the attentions of man. Domestic animals are kept in sheltered paddocks, (top) in Florida and (facing page bottom) in Kentucky, and have their mates chosen for them so as to produce particular types of offspring. Wild horses have to survive the rigors of the climate year-round and mate with any horse able to survive. Thus wild horses tend to produce animals suited to local conditions rather than human need. Above: Wild horses beside the Ross River in Australia. Facing page top: A wild herd in Wyoming. Overleaf: Semi-wild horses in New Mexico.

Polo, (above) the finals of the 1985 Coronation Cup, is the most entertaining equestrian sport to watch and the most difficult to master. The game consists of propelling a small ball with a bamboo mallet through goal posts 24 feet apart set at opposite ends of a 900 foot pitch. The game derives from a Persian and Indian game which was taken up by British army officers early in the 19th century. It was they who first formalized the rules and introduced it to Western society. Western polo is now a highly organized sport with international championships and contests, though because of the high cost of good polo ponies it remains a sport for the wealthier members of society. Top: The close of an amateur steeplechase. Facing page: Captain Mark Phillips competing in the 1985 Chatsworth Event.

Previous pages: Exercising English Thoroughbreds on a frosty winter morning at Kingsclere, Berkshire. The most demanding and exciting equestrian sport is often considered to be the three day event. As its name suggests this sport is spread over a meeting lasting three days, with each day devoted to a different skill. On the first day a dressage competition takes place to test the rider's control of the horse. The second day involves an exciting cross-country ride (these pages) against the clock. The third day is devoted to show jumping. Various points are awarded for each day and the total is added up at the close of the third day to produce a winner.

Three day eventing, (these pages) the cross country section, derived from training events for military riders and horses. War horses needed to be able to respond quickly to instructions from the rider and to be able to cope with any type of terrain which might be encountered during hostilities. These two demands created dressage and cross-country respectively, though originally there was no set pattern to dressage and only natural obstacles on the cross-country. In 1902 an event was held in Paris which combined all three skills, together with steeplechasing over a three day meeting. At first entry was restricted to army officers, as the contest was considered an extension of cavalry training, but gradually civilians were allowed to compete.

Top: Helen Ogden negotiates a hazardous water obstacle on Streetfighter in the 1986 Badminton Horse Trials. Badminton is generally recognized as the premier Three Day Event and attracts competitors from around the globe. The competition began in 1949 when the Duke of Beaufort laid out a cross-country course in the grounds of his Gloucestershire home, Badminton Park, after viewing the Olympic course set up at the British Army base at Aldershot the previous year. Above: Cynthia Ishoy on Dynasty during the 1988 Olympics. Facing page: The water jump at Burghley in 1987.

Previous pages: Horses graze contentedly in Connecticut. Mustangs (these pages and overleaf) are often considered the wild horse of North America, but such a view is misleading. Although the horse first evolved on the open plains of North America before spreading to Eurasia, it became extinct several thousand years ago. When the Spanish conquistadores arrived, they found a land empty of horses. It was when Spanish mounts escaped into the wild and began breeding that the American wild horse came into being. The Mustang is, therefore, a domestic horse in ancestry with a heavy Spanish influence. Later settlers crossed Mustangs with their own horses, adding Andalusian blood to their own stock to create specifically American breeds, such as the Quarterhorse.

Spain has produced a number of excellent horse breeds (these pages), which have added quality to other breeds with which they have been crossed. The most famous, and most highly prized, is the Andalusian Horse which has an elegant stride and outline which has made it a favorite for show work. The Hispano is about 16 hands, about the same as the Andalusian, but it is less Spanish, having large amounts of English Thoroughbred blood in its ancestry. The smaller Balearic Pony originates on the Balearic Islands of Majorca and Minorca where it is used for general agricultural work.

The domestic horse ranges widely in size and temperament between various breeds. The New Forest Pony (top) is rarely over 14 hands which, together with its intelligence and sure-footedness, makes it an ideal horse for children. The Arab (above and facing page top) stands 15 hands tall and is a lithe, elegant creature noted for its speed, endurance and courage. It makes a magnificent racing horse and has been used to improve the stock of many other breeds. The Shire (facing page bottom) is much heavier and stands over 17 hands. It is a slow mover but is immensely strong and has long been used for agricultural and draught work.

These pages: The Lippizaner herd at the Szilvasvarad Stud in Hungary. This small herd is one of the rare Lippizaner concentrations outside of Austria. The Hungarians, while maintaining a pure strain of the Lippizaners for stud, do not use them for dressage, as do the Austrians, but cross breed them with local horses to produce useful agricultural and draught horses which can be trained to a high level of proficiency.

PHOTOGRAPHERS' INDEX